Books by Frank Bidart

Golden State (1973)

The Book of the Body (1977)

The Book of the Body

The Book of the Body
Frank Bidart

Farrar, Straus and Giroux

New York

"The Arc" first appeared in *American Review* and "Ellen West" first appeared in *Ploughshares*. "Ellen West" is based on Ludwig Binswanger's *Der Fall Ellen West*, as translated by Werner M. Mendel and Joseph Lyons, included in *Existence*, edited by Rollo May, Ernest Angel, and Henri F. Ellenberger, copyright © 1958 by Basic Books, Inc., Publishers, New York.

Library of Congress Cataloging in Publication Data

Bidart, Frank   The Book of the Body

I. Title   PS3552.I33B6   811'.5'4   76-45853

Contents

The Book of the Body

The Arc

When I wake up,
                    I try to convince myself that my arm
isn't there—
             to retain my sanity.

Then I try to convince myself it is.

•   •   •

INSTRUCTIONS

1. Always bandage *firmly*. The pressure should be constant over the entire stump with greatest pressure near the tip to attempt to make the stump cone-shaped.

2. If stump starts to *throb*, remove the bandage at once. Leave bandage off for one hour and rebandage the stump as before, *firmly*. Inspect the skin of your stump daily for any blisters, spots or sores and report them.

3. Wash bandage with mild soap in luke warm water. DO NOT WRING! Squeeze the waters out gently and place the bandage over the shower rod to dry thoroughly. DO NOT STRETCH OR IRON!!

4. Change the stump sock daily. Wash the sock daily with mild soap in luke warm water. DO NOT WRING! Squeeze the water out gently—place the sock on a flat surface to dry.

•   •   •

I used to vaguely perceive the necessity
of coming to terms with the stump-filled, material world,—

things; bodies;
            CRAP—

a world of accident, and chance—;

but after
the accident, I had to understand it

not as an accident—;

                    the way my mother,
years before locked in McLean's,

believed the painting of a snow-scene above her bed
had been placed there by the doctor to make her feel cold.

How could we *convince* her it had no point?. . .

It had no point,—
                it was there
without relation to my mother; by chance; by
CHANCE the car swerved when a yellow car

came at us—; and the next
minute, when I looked down

all I saw was a space below the elbow
                            instead of my arm . . .

The police still can't figure out exactly what happened.

I tell myself:
"Insanity is the insistence on meaning."

•   •   •

He asked me if I wanted to get undressed, but I'm
embarrassed to take my shirt off,

so I told him to go ahead and take all his clothes off.

His body looked small and white lying on top of the dark bedspread.

I said I wanted to watch him wash
his prick.
   He got up and walked
to the washbasin against the wall,

then I went up, and started to wash
it with mild soap in luke warm water.
I squeezed it.
   He laughed,

and after drying off, went back to the bed.

I asked if he had a job.
     "Drove a truck for a while,
but about a week ago—I got laid off."

He looked uneasy, almost scared.
     "When I was in Vietnam,

my wife met someone else, and divorced me.
I have a little daughter three years old."

He got his wallet and showed me the little girl's picture.

"I don't blame my wife—I was gone
a long time, and like everybody
else in Vietnam I did a lot of fucking around."

He looked frightened and embarrassed, seeming to want
me to reassure him . . .
                    I asked him to tell me about Vietnam.

"Anything you touched might explode. I know guys
just kicked a rock, and got killed . . .
                            Once a buddy of mine
was passing a hut, when a gook motioned to him to come inside.
Inside a woman was lying on her back, with
a pile of cigarettes next to her. He threw
some cigarettes on the pile, got on top of her,
and shoved in his prick.
                    He screamed.
She had a razor blade inside.

The whole end of his thing was sliced in two . . .

They fixed it up;
                    but what can he tell his wife?"

When he asked me what kind of sex I wanted,
I suddenly

forgot why

a body can make me feel horny—;

I wanted to leave.
                    But afraid
leaving might insult him, I asked him to masturbate.

"Sure."
          He closed his eyes. For several minutes
his arm and hand with great energy
worked, as his contorted face tried to concentrate.

I stared at him, wishing
I could know
the image in his mind when at last he came.

                •   •   •

The person I can't forget on my mother's ward
I don't know the name of.
                          She still stands there
in my mind,—

              though it is summer, and hot,
she is wearing a heavy terry-cloth robe,
sweating, with a thin metal chain around her neck:

that's all—
          she is assuring me
she wears nothing under the robe,

that to wear anything
would *limit* her, that the doctors tell her
to have an "identity"
                    she must wear something—

7

"But I don't want an identity!

This way I'm *free* . . . Everybody else
has a medal on their chain, with a picture

or name on it, but I don't—
this way
I'm not bound down . . ."

With two hands
she begins to work the chain
around and around her neck, she soon gets
franticly excited,
                    and finally the attendant leads her away . . .

I only saw her once; that's
her identity in my mind,—

and even in my mind,

sweating
she wears a body.

•   •   •

In Michelangelo's drawing *The Dream*, a man,

his arms lightly touching the globe,
all the masks at last lying dead beneath him,

is wakened by an angel
                    hovering above him,

the angel's trumpet directed by the angel's arms,
the two figures connected by the trumpet,

wakened to the World ranged round him,
which is his dream, as well as Sin:

Sex. Identity. History. Family.
Affection. Obsession. Chance.

                        —the seven
Deadly Sins, spirit
implicating itself in matter, only able to know itself
by what it has done in Time,—

are all ranged round him, the angel
waking him to himself . . . his arms lightly touching the globe.

                    •   •   •

In Paris, on the footbridge between the Île St. Louis
and the Île de la Cité,

about six months after the accident,
I had an illumination:

the *solution* was to forget
that I had ever had an arm.
                    The lost arm had never existed.

Since the accident,
I had gotten more and more obsessed: the image
of what I had been,
                the anticipations,

9

demands and predilections of a two-armed man
haunted me—

I was no longer whole; proportioned; inviolate . . .

In a store, I found a "memorial album":
birth date, death date, place
of rest, visitors to the coffin—
                              I could clearly see
an obituary:
                    On a certain date, in a certain place,
                    he lost his arm.

Twice I dreamed the cone of my stump
was a gravestone:
                    I *saw* it:
                              the whole of my life
was a kind of arc
stretching between two etched, ineradicable dates . . .

I had to escape that arc—

even notions like *career* and *marriage* (all those things
which because they
have a beginning, must end—)
                              seemed to suffocate . . .

I went to Paris. My family's sympathy,
the vivid scenes of my former life

whispered that my body was bound by two iron dates . . .

One day, leaving my hotel on the Île St. Louis,
I saw a black dog and a young boy madly running.

Nothing unusual—
                    except the dog only had one
front leg. He seemed without consciousness
of what he lacked;
                    free of memory as a vegetable.

Looking at each other, they happily jogged along,
started to cross the bridge, and I followed—

then, as I crossed it, suddenly
I felt that I too must erase my past,
that I could, *must* pretend (almost
as an experiment) I had never had more
than one arm, that the image
faced in the mirror
was the only, the inevitable image . . .

—For a time, it worked;
                    I *was* happy;

without a past, I seemed not to exist
in time at all,—

I only remember a sense of release, ease,
proportion—
          I am now one, not less than one . . .

Then, after about two weeks, imperceptibly
everything I saw became

cardboard . . .

Even the things I touched—
                    I couldn't allow myself to remember

the vivid associations
which gave dimension to what I
                                    touched, saw, smelt,—

the resonance of every image
I had to try to cut from my brain, it had been felt
by someone with two hands and two arms . . .

I had to try to cut from my brain
                                    my phantom hand
which still gets cramps, which my brain still
recognizes as real—

                    and now, I think of Paris,

how Paris is still the city of Louis XVI and
Robespierre, how blood, amputation, and rubble

give her dimension, resonance, and grace.

Happy Birthday

Thirty-three, goodbye—
the awe I feel

is not that you won't come again, or why—

or even that after
a time, we think of those who are dead

with a sweetness that cannot be explained—

but that I've read the trading-cards:
RALPH TEMPLE CYCLIST CHAMPION TRICK RIDER

WILLIE HARRADON CYCLIST
THE YOUTHFUL PHENOMENON

F. F. IVES CYCLIST
100 MILES 6 H. 25 MIN. 30 SEC.

—as the fragile metal of their
wheels stopped turning, as they

took on wives, children, accomplishments, all those
predilections which also insisted on ending,

they could not tell themselves from what they had done.

Terrible to dress in the clothes
of a period that must end.

They didn't plan it that way—
they didn't plan it that way.

Elegy

I. BELAFONT

"He seemed to have gotten better—

    Tuesday, for the first time
    in a week, he went out
    into the front yard, and
    pottied by lifting his leg—

    which he hadn't had

    the strength to do. So we left him

    just for an hour—

    the vet says
    somebody must have
    got to him again, in
    that hour—

        one in the morning, he started to
        cough, throw up, and Floyd
        stayed with him
        all night—

        at six, he called the vet, and at ten
        he died.

He had a *good* life—

       you feel so guilty, even though you
       did all you could—

              I talked
              to my doctor, and

       he says you
       always feel that way, though you
       did all you
       humanly could—all you
       humanly could—"

(*pause*) "He had a *good* life—"

              My mother's dog is dead;
              as truly as I am, he was her son;
              we used to laugh at the comparison.

"When your father was drunk one night,
he started to hit me; you were only five, but
stood up to him, and said:
              'If you ever
try to hit mommy again, I'll kill you.'

I knew then I *had* to leave.

When we came to the city,
you were a real toughie—

I'll never forget the first
day of kindergarten, you were sent home because
you called the lady teacher a 'sonofabitch'!

—You'd only been around cowboys;
but later, you only wanted to be with me.

I had to *push* you away—

we were always
more like each other than anyone else."

                        We used to laugh at the comparison.

"I insisted they bury him here, in the garden: Floyd
made a box: we wrapped him

in one of our best
white sheets."—Was it his fault

they loved him
more than each other? Or their fault

their love
forbade him in his nine years

from even licking his genitals?
She got him

the year before I went away to school,
"to take your place,"

she kidded. She used to laugh
at poodles on the street—clipped, manicured,

clung to.
But what was she to do—

change, or have another child?

        Belafont, I saw you in a dream tonight,
        reaching toward me to kiss me

        but carefully avoiding the mouth, as
        taught,

        yet constantly, defiantly skirting it—
        then plunging into a pile of old, empty shoeboxes

        to come up with the strap
        I wear on my weak

        left wrist
        exercising each night, remaking

        the embarrassing
        soft overfed unloved body

        I try to blame on the past—;
        tilting your head, the strap

        hanging from one side of the mouth,
        you look at me with your

daring, lawless
stare—

and begin to chew.

II. PRUNING

"I'd rather die than let them
take off a breast. I'd rather die
than go through cobalt again."

She means it,—
                        but I can't help but remember
her at least fifteen years earlier,

standing in the doorway, shrieking at me
when I wanted to be a priest:
                        "It's just as well!

You had mumps—; they went down—; you'll never,
gelding, have kids!"
                        twisting her last knife

to save me from the Church, the Church
which called her remarriage adultery . . .

—She is saying: "If the cancer
pops out somewhere else, I won't let them operate.
I'd rather die.
                        They just
butcher you . . . Besides, it never works."

III. LOVER

"I'll be right over."
"Give me a few minutes: I'm still

in my pajamas."
"Don't get out of your pajamas."

"Don't get out of my pajamas?"
"—Don't get out of your pajamas!"

And so we learned how to make two lovers
of friends; now,

caught "between a rock and a hard place—" (after
the hospital, after

"gestation" was "interrupted") we still
when we call even say we love each other . . .

Too bad two people don't have to "love each other"
more, to make a child.

IV. LIGHT

I am asleep, dreaming a terrible dream, so I awake,
and want to call my father to ask if, just
for a short time, the dog can come to stay with me.

But the light next to my bed won't light:
I press and press the switch. Touching the phone,
I can't see to dial the numbers. Can I learn how to keep

the dog in my apartment? In the dark, trying
a second light, I remember
I always knew these machines would fail me.
                                        Then I awake,

remember my father and the dog are dead,
the lights in that room do not go on.

V . LINEAGE

"I went to a mausoleum today, and found
what I want. Eye-level.
Don't forget:
I want to be buried in a mausoleum at eye-level."

She feels she never quite recovered
from her mother's, my grandmother's, death.

Her mother died by falling from a
third floor hospital window.

"—I'm *sure* she didn't want to kill herself;

after the stroke, sometimes she got confused, and
maybe she thought
                             she saw grandpa at the window . . .

She wanted to be at home. After the stroke,
we *had* to put her in a nursing home,—

she hated it, but you couldn't
get help to stay with her, and she needed
someone twenty-four hours a day,—

she begged me to take her out;
                                            the cruel,
unreasonable things she said to me! Her doctor

told me I was doing the right thing, but
what she said
                almost drove me crazy . . .

it's astonishing how clearly I can still hear her voice.

I still dream I can see her falling
three stories, her arms stretching out . . .

For forty years, she counted
on grandpa,—
                after he died, she still
talked to him.

I know I made a lot of
mistakes with you, but I couldn't count on anyone—

I had to be both father *and* mother . . ."

As the subject once again changes from my grandmother

to my father, or the dog—
to my stepfather, or me—
                her obsessive, baffled voice

says that when she allowed herself to love

she let something into her head which will
never be got out—;
                which could only betray her
or *be* betrayed, but never appeased—;
whose voice

      death and memory have made
into a razor-blade without a handle . . .

"Don't forget:
I want to be buried in a mausoleum at eye-level."

ENVOI

"If it resists me, I know it's real—"
a friend said. I thought of you . . . When I said,
"I feel too much. I can't stand what I feel"

I meant, as always, facing you.—You're real;
and smile at me no *less* woundedly, dead.
If it resists me, I know it's real.

Now no act of Mind,—or Will,—can reveal
the secret to *un-say* all we once said . . .
I feel too much. I can't stand what I feel.

The only way we stumbled to the Real
was through failure; outrage; betrayals; dread.
If it resists me, I know it's real.

Is the only salvation through what's real?
But each book . . . reads me—; who remains unread.
I feel too much. I can't stand what I feel.

Mother, I didn't forgive you. Conceal
unreal forgiving. Show me your face in fury—; not dead.
If it resists me, I know it's real.
I feel too much. I can't stand what I feel.

The Book of the Body

Wanting to cease to feel—;

since 1967,
so much blood under the bridge,—

the deaths of both my parents,
(now that they have no
body, only when I have no body

can we meet—)

my romance with Orgasm,

exhilaration like Insight, but without
content?—

the NO which is YES, the YES which is NO—

Daphnis,
astonished at the unaccustomed threshold of heaven,

in his whiteness
sees beneath his feet the clouds and stars . . .

—So many
infatuations guaranteed to fail before they started,

terror at my own homosexuality,

terror which somehow
evaporated slowly with "Gay Liberation"

and finding that I had fathered a child—;

. . . All those who loved me
whom I did not want;

all those whom I loved
who did not want me;

all those whose love I reciprocated

but in a way somehow
                        unlike what they wanted . . .

—Blindness. Blankness.
A friend said, "I've hurt so many . . ." And

for what?
               to what *end?*—

An adult's forgiveness of his parents
born out of increasing age and empathy

which really forgives nothing,—
but is loathing, rage, revenge,

yet forgiveness as well—;

Sex the type of all action,

reconciliation with the body that is
annihilation of the body,

28

My romance with pornography,

watching it happen, watching

two bodies trying to make it happen,
however masterful or gorgeous, helpless

climbing the un-mappable mountain
of FEELING, the will

in sweat, hurt, exhaustion, accepting
limits of will,

the NO which is YES, the YES which is NO.

1974.

Ellen West

I love sweets,—
                    heaven
would be dying on a bed of vanilla ice cream . . .

But my true self
is thin, all profile

and effortless gestures, the sort of blond
elegant girl whose
                    body is the image of her soul.

—My doctors tell me I must give up
this ideal;
            but I
WILL NOT . . . cannot.

Only to my husband I'm not simply a "case."

But he is a fool. He married
meat, and thought it was a wife.

                         ●   ●   ●

Why am I a girl?

I ask my doctors, and they tell me they
don't know, that it is just "given."

But it has such
implications—;
                    and sometimes,
I even feel like a girl.

                    •   •   •

Now, at the beginning of Ellen's thirty-second year, her physical
condition has deteriorated still further. Her use of laxatives in-
creases beyond measure. Every evening she takes sixty to seventy
tablets of a laxative, with the result that she suffers tortured vomit-
ing at night and violent diarrhea by day, often accompanied by a
weakness of the heart. She has thinned down to a skeleton, and
weighs only 92 pounds.

                    •   •   •

About five years ago, I was in a restaurant,
eating alone
                    with a book. I was
not married, and often did that . . .

—I'd turn down
dinner invitations, so I could eat alone;

I'd allow myself two pieces of bread, with
butter, at the beginning, and three scoops of
vanilla ice cream, at the end,—

                              sitting there alone
with a book, both in the book
and out of it, waited on, idly
watching people,—

when an attractive young man
and woman, both elegantly dressed,
sat next to me.
                    She was beautiful—;

with sharp, clear features, a good
bone structure—;
                    if she took her make-up off
in front of you, rubbing cold cream
again and again across her skin, she still would be
beautiful—
                    more beautiful.

And he,—
                    I couldn't remember when I had seen a man
so attractive. I didn't know why. He was almost

a male version
                    of her,—

I had the sudden, mad notion that I
wanted to be his lover . . .

—Were they married?
                    were *they* lovers?

They didn't wear wedding rings.

Their behavior was circumspect. They discussed
politics. They didn't touch . . .

—How could I discover?

Then, when the first course
arrived, I noticed the way

each held his fork out for the other

to taste what he had ordered . . .

They did this
again and again, with pleased looks, indulgent
smiles, for each course,
                    more than once for *each* dish—;
much too much for just friends . . .

—Their behavior somehow sickened me;

the way each *gladly*
put the *food* the other had offered *into his mouth*—;

I knew what they were. I knew they slept together.

An immense depression came over me . . .

—I knew I could never
with such ease allow another to put food into my mouth:

happily *myself* put food into another's mouth—;

I knew that to become a wife I would have to give up my ideal.

•   •   •

Even as a child,
I saw that the "natural" process of aging

is for one's middle to thicken—
one's skin to blotch;

as happened to my mother.
And her mother.

I loathed "Nature."

At twelve, pancakes
became the most terrible thought there is . . .

I shall *defeat* "Nature."

In the hospital, when they
weigh me, I wear weights secretly sewn into my belt.

       ●   ●   ●

January 16. The patient is allowed to eat in her room, but comes readily with her husband to afternoon coffee. Previously she had stoutly resisted this on the ground that she did not really eat but devoured like a wild animal. This she demonstrated with utmost realism. . . . Her physical examination showed nothing striking. Salivary glands are markedly enlarged on both sides.

January 21. Has been reading *Faust* again. In her diary, writes that art is the "mutual permeation" of the "world of the body" and the "world of the spirit." Says that her own poems are "hospital poems . . . weak—without skill or perseverance; only managing to beat their wings softly."

February 8. Agitation, quickly subsided again. Has attached herself to an elegant, very thin female patient. Homo-erotic component strikingly evident.

February 15. Vexation, and torment. Says that her mind forces her always to think of eating. Feels herself degraded by this. Has entirely, for the first time in years, stopped writing poetry.

•   •   •

Callas is my favorite singer, but I've only
seen her once—;

I've never forgotten that night . . .

—It was in *Tosca*, she had long before
lost weight, her voice
had been, for years,
                    deteriorating, half itself . . .

When her career began, of course, she was fat,

enormous—; in the early photographs,
sometimes I almost don't recognize her . . .

The voice too then was enormous—

healthy; robust; subtle; but capable of
crude effects, even vulgar,
                    almost out of
high spirits, too much health . . .

But soon she felt that she must lose weight,—
that all she was trying to express

was obliterated by her body,
buried in flesh—;
                    abruptly, within
four months, she lost at least sixty pounds . . .

—The gossip in Milan was that Callas
had swallowed a tapeworm.

But of course she hadn't.

                        The *tapeworm*
was her *soul* . . .

—How her soul, uncompromising,
insatiable,
                must have loved eating the flesh from her bones,

revealing this extraordinarily
mercurial; fragile; masterly creature . . .

—But irresistibly, nothing
stopped there; the huge voice

also began to change: at first, it simply diminished
in volume, in size,
                        then the top notes became
shrill, unreliable—at last,
usually not there at all . . .

—No one knows *why*. Perhaps her mind,
ravenous, still insatiable, sensed

that to struggle with the *shreds* of a voice

must make her artistry subtler, more refined,
more capable of expressing humiliation,
rage, betrayal . . .

—Perhaps the opposite. Perhaps her spirit
loathed the unending struggle

to *embody* itself, to *manifest* itself, on a stage whose

mechanics, and suffocating customs,
seemed expressly designed to annihilate spirit . . .

—I know that in *Tosca*, in the second act,
when, humiliated, hounded by Scarpia,
she sang V*issi d'arte*
                    —"I lived for art"—

and in torment, bewilderment, at the end she asks,
with a voice reaching
                    harrowingly for the notes,

"Art has *repaid* me LIKE THIS?"

                              I felt I was watching
autobiography—
                    an art; skill;
virtuosity

miles distant from the usual soprano's
athleticism,—
                    the usual musician's dream
of virtuosity *without* content . . .

—I wonder what she feels, now,
listening to her recordings.

For they have already, within a few years,
begun to date . . .

Whatever they express
they express through the style of a decade
and a half—;
                    a style *she* helped create . . .

—She must know that now
she probably would *not* do a trill in
exactly that way,—
                  that the whole sound, atmosphere,
dramaturgy of her recordings

have just slightly become those of the past . . .

—Is it bitter? Does her soul
tell her

that she was an *idiot* ever to think
anything
          material wholly could satisfy?. . .

—Perhaps it says: *The only way*
to escape
the History of Styles

is not to have a body.

                   ●   ●   ●

When I open my eyes in the morning, my great
mystery
          stands before me . . .

—I *know* that I am intelligent; therefore

the inability not to fear food
day-and-night; this unending hunger
ten minutes after I have eaten . . .
                              a childish
dread of eating; hunger which can have no cause,—

half my mind says that all this
is *demeaning* . . .

              Bread
for days on end
drives all real thought from my brain . . .

—Then I think, No. The ideal of being thin

conceals the ideal
not to have a body—;
                which is NOT trivial . . .

This wish seems now as much a "given" of my existence

as the intolerable
fact that I am dark-complexioned; big-boned;
and once weighed
one hundred and sixty-five pounds . . .

—But then I think, No. That's too simple,—

without a body, who can
know himself at all?
              Only by
acting; choosing; rejecting; have I
made myself—
            discovered who and what *Ellen* can be . . .

—But then again I think, NO. This *I* is anterior

to name; gender; action;
fashion;
       MATTER ITSELF,—

. . . trying to stop my hunger with FOOD
is like trying to appease thirst

with ink.

•   •   •

March 30. Result of the consultation: Both gentlemen agree com-
pletely with my prognosis and doubt any therapeutic usefulness of
commitment even more emphatically than I. All three of us are
agreed that it is not a case of obsessional neurosis and not one of
manic-depressive psychosis, and that no definitely reliable therapy
is possible. We therefore resolved to give in to the patient's demand
for discharge.

•   •   •

The train-ride yesterday
was far *worse* than I expected . . .

In our compartment
were ordinary people: a student;
a woman; her child;—

they had ordinary bodies, pleasant faces;

but I thought
I was surrounded by creatures

with the pathetic, desperate
desire to be *not* what they were:—

the student was short,
and carried his body as if forcing
it to be taller—;

the woman showed her gums when she smiled,
and often held her
hand up to hide them—;

the child
seemed to cry simply because it was
small; a dwarf, and helpless . . .

—I was hungry. I had insisted that my husband
not bring food . . .

After about thirty minutes, the woman
peeled an orange

to quiet the child. She put a section
into its mouth—;
                    immediately it spit it out.

The piece fell to the floor.

—She pushed it with her foot through the dirt
toward me
several inches.

My husband saw me staring
down at the piece . . .

—I didn't move; how I wanted
to reach out,
                    and as if invisible

shove it in my mouth—;

my body
became rigid. As I stared at him,
I could see him staring

at me,—

        then he looked at the student—; at the woman—; then
back to me . . .

I didn't move.

—At last, he bent down, and
casually

        threw it out the window.

He looked away.

—I got up to leave the compartment, then
saw his face,—

his eyes
were red;

        and I saw

—*I'm sure I saw*—

disappointment.

                    •   •   •

On the third day of being home she is as if transformed. At break-
fast she eats butter and sugar, at noon she eats so much that—for
the first time in thirteen years!—she is satisfied by her food and gets
really full. At afternoon coffee she eats chocolate creams and Easter

eggs. She takes a walk with her husband, reads poems, listens to recordings, is in a positively festive mood, and all heaviness seems to have fallen away from her. She writes letters, the last one a letter to the fellow patient here to whom she had become so attached. In the evening she takes a lethal dose of poison, and on the following morning she is dead. "She looked as she had never looked in life—calm and happy and peaceful."

•   •   •

Dearest.—I remember how
at eighteen,
                on hikes with friends, when
they rested, sitting down to joke or talk,

I circled
around them, afraid to hike ahead alone,

yet afraid to rest
when I was not yet truly thin.

You and, yes, my husband,—
you and he

have by degrees drawn me within the circle;
forced me to sit down at last on the ground.

I am grateful.

But something in me *refuses* it.

—How eager I have been
to compromise, to kill this *refuser*,—

but each compromise, each attempt
to poison an ideal
which often seemed to *me* sterile and unreal,

heightens my hunger.

I am crippled. I disappoint you.

Will you greet with anger, or
happiness,

the news which might well reach you
before this letter?

    Your *Ellen.*